SURVIVOR

a journey through abortion and back

SHEILA HARPER

New York

for Meghan

DEFINITION

Survivor:
The one of two or more people,
as joint tenants,
who outlives the other
or others.

GRATITUDE

To Hoyt and Marcheta Fitzsimmons,
for without your constant presence in my life
I could not have survived.
Thank you for the firm foundation
upon which you have shown me how to live.

OUR STORY BEGINS

with me as a 19-year old college freshman, very much in love with my boyfriend, "Brian." I appeared to be a good girl, one who could make smart decisions, who was dependable, and showed respect for others. I was known to be able to discern between right and wrong---except in the area of my physical relationship with my boyfriend, with whom I chose to be sexually active. I loved Brian very much, and I liked our life together. But I knew I was not ready to have a child. Since I wasn't ignorant about what could happen, I made sure we were "careful" so I wouldn't get pregnant and have to worry about one more thing while I was in college. I was having a great time, and everything seemed to be under control. But I quickly learned that I couldn't control everything when I found out that our physical relationship had produced my pregnancy.

It was at this point that I had a predicament. What was I to do? On my quest for answers, I decided to tell Brian. I knew he would share my burden and agree that we could not have a child at this point. You can imagine my dismay and shock when I saw him become excited at the thought of us having a child together.

Still, *nothing* in me wanted this to happen. I ventured on to find an answer I wanted to hear. I told my best friend and she immediately told me how easy her abortion at 15 was, that it was no big deal. Now this was an answer I could accept. I wanted to hear how I could solve this problem quickly and secretively so I could get back to living the good life. Abortion definitely appeared to be the answer.

When I told Brian of my decision he was distraught. He cried, begged, and pleaded for me to change my mind. My only thought was that he had lost his mind or that he was still excited about having a baby and wasn't thinking clearly. I knew in a few weeks he would thank me because our problem would be solved and we could start having a good time once again. This would be just a little obstacle, something that we could get through together.

He evidently didn't want to hear any more of my plan, because he began making plans for marriage, while I made an appointment at the abortion clinic. Meanwhile, his family attempted to persuade me to change my mind. Change my mind?! What were they trying to do? Sabotage my future? They didn't realize what they were asking. Brian and I had the rest of our lives together, so we could have our first child when we were ready and mature enough to raise one. And why was he making my decision for me? It was my body, and he wasn't going to dictate what I did to it.

But despite all my oppositions to his pleas, I wondered about the feelings of Brian and his family. Why was this upsetting them so much? Why was I still uneasy? Was there more to an abortion than I realized? My best friend had an abortion and she seemed fine. But then I also had a friend in high school who had never recovered after her abortion at 16. I shook those thoughts out of my head.

When I would lie in my bed at night, I would place my hand on my stomach and allow myself a moment to dream about what was developing inside me. Was this really a baby? Is it supposed to be born? No, certainly not. "Abortion is okay," I would tell myself. Why else would it be legal? The Supreme Court is comprised of well-educated minds, people who have probably researched and debated the topic extensively. I could just imagine them weighing the pros and cons, flipping through statistics, and then announcing to America its new freedom. I began to think that the experts had already solved my abortion dilemma, so I had nothing further to ponder.

MARCH 29, 1985

was the day I had scheduled for my abortion. Brian showed up at my apartment that morning urging me to reconsider. I assured him I was making the best, logical decision for both of us. But inside, I was queasy, dreading to face my decision. Something inside was screaming for me to stop, but why I didn't pay attention, I will never know. Instead, I plowed on, certain I was making the right choice. I kept the picture of the Supreme Court in my mind. They were the highest form of law and justice, so their judgment on the issue had obviously been the result of a majority rule. They were right and my longing to deviate from my plan and their judgment was wrong. I was probably just being overemotional.

When I heard my best friend's tires stop on the gravel outside, I knew it was time to follow through with my decision. The instant Brian heard the same sound he began to cry. He asked for the final time to put a stop to my plan as I went out the door. Honestly, I wanted him to physically stop me. I wanted someone to help me, to provide alternatives other than getting married and having the baby. I also wanted to be doing anything else on this day besides having an abortion.

HAVING AN ABORTION

is not a normal little girl's dream. It's never mentioned in the fairy tales, and it's certainly not the "happily ever after" ending. My "happily ever after" began when I walked the aisle of a little country Baptist church and became a genuine believer in Jesus Christ. This was a serious decision for me, even at the age of twelve.

I recall as I was eating breakfast one morning before

school, my older sister told me that she had been "saved" the night before at a revival. As she was telling me about her experience, I was certain that was what I needed. God should be in my life. He was what I had been missing. I could hardly pay attention in school all day because I couldn't wait to go to this "revival" she talked about (whatever a revival was, I had no idea).

Her friend picked us up for church that night. When we arrived at the church, I was so excited to get "saved" that I didn't pay a bit of attention to what the preacher said all evening. Nor do I even remember who was preaching. I just remember that when he gave the opportunity for people to come forward and get "saved", I was the first one walking down the aisle. I knew that Christ was what my heart demanded and I was not leaving without Him.

My life after that night totally changed. I began to commit myself to this newfound relationship with Jesus. It offered me a freedom and a peace that I had never known before. I became very involved in the youth group at that little Baptist church and loved it. When evangelists came to town I would be the first one to volunteer to work at the altars, where I would help lead people to know the same Christ I knew. I cherished being able to see kids my age experience that same transformation and find the freedom I had found. I wanted to witness it over and over firsthand. Anytime there was a special day of bringing visitors to church I always brought a pew full. When there was a Bible challenge, I wanted to be the first to get the answer right. I loved the Lord with all my heart and vowed to myself and to God that I would live for Him all the days of my life.

Or at least until college, which was where I broke

that vow. I discovered that the youth group had been my safety net. As soon as I got away from it, I started straying because I no longer had the much-needed accountability and encouragement of my Christian friends. Unfortunately, my relationship with God was really shallow. The moment a distraction came along I forgot all the meaningful things I had learned and how much they meant to me.

So preparing for an abortion at 19 was certainly not a day I thought I would ever face. I can still vividly see me looking through the back window of my friend's car at Brian, fallen to his knees, weeping uncontrollably. My heart was breaking. I never imagined I could ever do anything to hurt someone that deeply, especially someone I loved. I wanted to jump out and run back to him, but I knew I couldn't because I would still be faced with this problem. I knew one day he would be grateful that we didn't wreck our lives so young.

In silence, we drove to the bank, where I cashed a check for $250 to pay for the abortion. I had saved every penny because Brian refused to pay for any of it. Another moment I remember so vividly is when the teller passed the money through the window. Once I had the money in my hand, the gravity of the situation settled on me; there was no turning back to anywhere, for now I was headed to a destination that would change my life forever.

I DON'T REMEMBER

the drive to the abortion clinic in Chattanooga, TN. My friend gave me some pills to calm me. It was the first time I had ever taken a drug, but my anxiety seemed to warrant the occasion for any kind of relief.

We drove through the heavy line of protestors outside the clinic and my friend and I hurried inside. What was that horrid smell? I told the receptionist my name was "Sally" something and she confirmed my appointment. After a few minutes I was given a form to fill out, but I don't remember writing anything. I just knew that when I took the paper back to the receptionist she told me that I would be called back for my counseling any minute. Counseling? COUNSELING? I was going to get COUNSELING? That was the most positive word I had heard the past week or so! Counseling. I was really going to get counseling. Someone that was older than me, that knew about the process that understood my feelings, was going to give me an alternative. I tried to hear every word the receptionist said. I just knew that counseling was going to give me an avenue out of this horrible place. I was so excited. Why didn't I think to seek counseling from someone besides my best friend and my boyfriend?

"Sally!"

Oooh, that's me! "I'll be back in a minute--I'm going for my counseling," I told my friend. I walked into the office and was awestruck by the person sitting on the opposite side of the desk. I had never seen someone more blank...dead...almost lifeless, but amazingly enough, still breathing. I was almost afraid of this woman. I was filled with emotions. This "counselor" didn't look like my idea of a trusted confidant. She wasn't even friendly. But I was still hopeful. Being able to just sit down released all the emotions I had kept inside since I had seen the positive sign on the pregnancy test. I was finally going to get to unload my feelings to someone who understood. I was sobbing as she asked in a monotone drawl, "Do you want to have this abortion?" I answered to the best of my ability, because by now I was an emotional wreck. I continued, "I don't know any other choice," thinking that was the answer she needed to wake up her compassion. "No other choice," she would think. Then she would pull out the agencies, the alternatives, the government assistance, whatever would show me a way out of there.

But she didn't. She took a 2 by 2-inch white card, wrote a '2' on it, and handed it back to me. Then she said, "Go sit down in the waiting room and they'll call your number in a minute." End of counseling. End of hope. I tried to compose myself and dry my tears before I left her office. I felt like I had just left an upright coffin.

A few more minutes passed and I was called back for a pregnancy test, which sure enough, proved me pregnant. Someone then led me to a locker room, where I exchanged my clothes for a hospital gown. I was then given a key to lock up my personal belongings. Then I walked into a room that had a wall of cubicles, one of which I sat behind to sign more papers. Then I was given more pills. Through yet another door and into a waiting room I sat beside another girl who seemed to be as alone as I was feeling. For more than an hour, we didn't look at each other nor did we talk. My head was swimming, and I saw that the room was getting smaller and smaller because it was filling up with more and more girls. There were girls sitting on every chair, every couch, and every arm of every couch and chair.

When the room was packed beyond capacity the doctor came in and told us the order of things. All I remember was that I needed to listen for the number "2" that the dead lady wrote on my little white card.

"Number one!"

Oh no...I'm next.

Thirty minutes passed.

"Number two!"

Here we go.

As I made my way through the maze of girls, forced to step over ones sitting on the floor, I could already smell the stench of vomit coming from the room in which I was entering.

"I'M DOING THE RIGHT THING,"

I told myself. Yes, I have a right to do the right thing. But if it's the right decision then why do I feel so dreadful? Why do I feel so dirty and shameful just for being here? Why does this doctor make me think of the devil? Why am I so scared? Why did I wish Brian had stopped me? Why did my friend in high school seem so different after her abortion? It's too late and I didn't have time to answer those lingering questions.

As I lie back on the cold, steel table, the nurse held my hand and told me everything was going to be "just fine." I put my feet in the stirrups and was covered so I wouldn't see what the doctor was doing down there. Instantly I felt the most pain I had ever felt before deep within me. I jumped and asked what the hurt was and the nurse said the doctor was dilating my cervix manually. I recalled my sister having a baby and we counted her centimeters of dilation as they were naturally increasing. What I was feeling was most definitely not natural, but forced by human instruments.

The nurse started counting: "That's one, that's two, that's three."

Something was terribly wrong. This pain, this agonizing pain was intentional, not natural. I never saw my sister writhe in pain during dilation.

"That's seven, that's eight."

Oh, my God, when is this going to end? Why am I doing this?

"Okay we're at ten now."

What's that sound? I heard a machine that sounded like a vacuum cleaner. It was so loud. Would I always remember that sound? At that moment, I knew what was happening, and I couldn't bear to think of what I was doing to my body and what was in it.

Almost as soon as it started the sound was gone. Two nurses tried to sit me upright and move me from the table because they had another patient coming in. I tried to stand up but my legs wouldn't carry me. My whole body was weak and shaky, so they had to carry me to the next waiting room. It was a room lined with beanbag chairs, one of which they placed me on to recover alone. Out of the corner of my eye I saw the girl that was sitting on the couch from earlier. "Why was she crying?" I wondered. And suddenly I realized I was crying too.

From where my beanbag chair was positioned I could see the entire room. I saw each girl from the packed waiting room wearily entering this new room with a different look in her eyes. There was something in them that I could see that I didn't want to recognize. Something in those eyes that made me want to look away in disgrace. But what was it? Why did I not want people to look at me, and why couldn't I look at anyone else?

The nurses told me to remain on the chair until I felt able to leave on my own. The drugs I had taken had not worn off yet, but I knew I was ready to leave. I found my locker and changed into my clothes. I found my friend and told her I just wanted to get out of there. I was handed a bunch of papers on my way out. We were met in the parking lot by yelling protestors. One tapped me on the shoulder and yelled in my face, "Do you know what you've just done?!" My friend shoved me in the car and took off. She went straight to my apartment and dropped me off. Brian was still there waiting for me.

He helped me to my bed, and listened as I explained the whole disturbing experience. Oddly enough, I was feeling better about it. Being back with him made everything okay again. I assured him once more that our lives would get back to normal as soon as I recovered. He listened in silence. That night, he drove to Wendy's and bought me a hamburger--another odd memory I have retained from that day.

I woke up the next morning to see Brian sleeping on the couch. I got up and got ready for work. I felt so good. In the shower I remember looking down at my stomach and literally thinking how happy I was that my worst problem was over. No one would ever need to know. Abortion really wasn't that bad after all. In fact, it was a piece of cake. On March 30, 1985, my emotions could be summed up in one word: Relief.

RELIEF

exuded from me. I went to work for the next several days knowing my mind and body were free. I kept my mind only on the fact that I wasn't pregnant anymore. The moment my mind tried to shift back to the clinic, the girls, the smell, and the sound of that machine, I would instantly think of something else. Eventually, that part of my experience will not even be a memory I thought. I was in the process of putting this whole experience behind me and moving ahead with school, work, and my boyfriend.

But I had noticed over the past week or so that Brian seemed quiet and distant. I assumed he was still angry and upset about the abortion. It was much better this way. He just had to realize that my decision was necessary for us to continue our lives together. He was never convinced, though, because after about two weeks, he told me he never wanted to see me again. I was devastated. I couldn't believe it. I knew why. He didn't even have to tell me. In fact, he didn't tell me. He just left.

Relief suddenly turned into pain, and almost regret. If I had to accept why he left, then I might have to accept what I did was an atrocity and I couldn't do that. I'll just show him that my life can go on when I turn up at our favorite spots with a new boyfriend. I knew a new boyfriend would occupy my mind. So I found a gorgeous man, a really good guy, someone I was proud to be going out with. I wondered if I should tell him that I had an abortion a few weeks earlier. No, that would not be a good idea. I felt shame for the first time, but brushed it off as being a ridiculous emotion.

My new good looking mind-occupier called me one day and asked if I could pick him up because he had to leave his car at the shop. Of course I said, "Yes," and went on my way. We were having a great time driving down the road when he hit the button to my glove compartment and it fell open. Into his lap fell all the papers from the abortion clinic, evidence of my secret in plain view. How they got in my glove compartment I will never know. He picked them up, looked at them, and then looked at me with a horrified expression that I had never seen before that day. I grabbed the papers, stuffed them in the compartment and shut it. I drove on and suddenly he made me pull the car over. I burst into tears and he comforted me, telling me everything would be all right.

We had made plans to meet and go to my grandparent's house the next night for an anniversary party. The following night I sat at the meeting location all by myself and was an hour late to the party. I knew why he didn't show up.

I made a decision that night that my secret would be locked up forever. This one choice had already forced me to be rejected by one person I cared deeply about and another I hardly knew. Something was terribly wrong. To what extent had I messed up my life? How was I ever going to fix this?

New clothes always made me feel better. So I started buying clothes. When I couldn't afford them anymore, I applied for a credit card. When I maxed out that credit card, I applied for another, then another, then another. When I couldn't get any more credit cards, I bought a new car that I couldn't afford.

The consumer market was exploding because of me, and because of it, I didn't focus on how much I had messed up my life.

Shopping helped alter my thinking during the day, but my mind still contained my experience in the evenings when I went home. So I attempted to get rid of the memories of March 29 by visiting bars, where no one cared what my secrets were. Because of my new sanity-saver I started drinking more, and then the nightmares started.

I WAS STANDING IN MY FAVORITE BAR

and Brian walked in. My stomach started rolling, literally like waves on the ocean. I looked down at it and he looked at me in horror. I fell over on a table and rolled over on my back. I was screaming in pain. Suddenly my stomach ripped open and its contents poured out all over the floor. Then I woke up sweating, and in agony.

What was happening to me? How was I going to get over this? Instead of my life getting easier and my pain more bearable, the event of March 29 was consuming me. I did not understand why, because it was the day that I was doing everything in my own power to forget.

By now the crowd I was hanging out with were all bar hoppers looking for a quick, good time. I fit right in. My best friend was still the same girl that took me to the abortion clinic. She had changed right along with me. One night in a drunken stupor I brought up my abortion. I so longed to talk about it with someone, anyone. I asked her if she ever thought about hers and if it ever bothered her. Even in our altered state of mind I remember her saying that her mother made her have an abortion at 15 and it bothered her so badly that she tried to commit suicide at 16. Why didn't she tell me that? I never knew the answer because that was the end of our friendship.

Months went by and I continued to support our economy through buying, drinking, and partying. I felt I was managing my addictions fairly well. The crowd I was with started using other drugs that I also used as a catalyst for my pain. Marijuana offered me a little more time to escape to a better place than where I was. It just seemed the next logical step as retribution for what I had done. I worked diligently to keep myself numb from the time I woke up until the time I went to bed. My drug use got so out of control that I couldn't really function unless I was chemically altered. I had to have something to make me wake up and to help me sleep, and I was dependent on liquor and pot for the times in-between. These substances made me numb, and if I kept myself numb, then not only could I avoid the thoughts of March 29, but the nightmares would come less often, and I couldn't hear the sound of that machine they used on the day that I thought my problems ended.

For a year after the abortion, my problems seemed to multiply. I saw absolutely no way out. My abortion was final. The only way to fix it was to recreate that dreadful day and make a different choice. Now that was something I couldn't do with any amount of drugs, will, or power.

I occasionally thought of God and wondered if He could fix this, but instantly knew there was no way He ever would accept me back. Not after what I had done. I was probably a monster to Him; too dirty, used, rejected, and definitely of no value to Him. So as I started thinking about my emptiness, I thought of a way out.

If I was going to have to live the rest of my life enduring this inward pain, the guilt, shame, and hurtful rejection, then there was no point in living. So I planned the day, I planned the method, and I commenced getting my affairs in order for the moment my life on Earth would end.

I LIED

and told everyone at work that I was sick. I had spent the evening before calling different family members and talking to them for a little while, telling them how much I loved them. I knew they would realize why I called when they got a phone call the next day. I shared an apartment with my stepsister, so I prepared her and her boyfriend dinner that night. It was my little way of saying bye and telling her how much I loved her.

As I drove home from work in the middle of the day everything seemed so surreal. I couldn't believe all I was doing was being done for the last time. I was very sad and shaken. How did I let my one choice change my life so drastically? Wasn't I the little girl that used to enjoy leading people to Christ and seeing their lives get better? What happened to that little girl who loved Christ?

I went to my stepsister's room, opened her nightstand drawer, and retrieved her pistol. I didn't want to waste any time, I just wanted to get this over with. I walked to the couch. I turned the gun around, steadied the butt of it against my fingers, and put both my thumbs on the trigger. I leaned over and placed the cold, steel barrel between my eyes and sat for what seemed like an eternity trying to let go of my nerves and catch my strength. I was crying so loudly and remember seeing my tears splash on our dusty hardwood floor. I started talking to myself saying, "Just do it! JUST DO IT!" I couldn't seem to muster the courage, so I decided that the easiest way to just do it would be to pull the trigger slowly. That way I wouldn't know when the bullet released, and then this nightmare would finally be over. So that's what I did. Slowly, in total silence and without a breath, I began to pull the trigger.

The silence was broken by the sound of tires on the gravel in my driveway. It startled me so much, I ran to the window to see who was there, only to see my stepsister home in the middle of the day. That moment was the first time I had thought about what her coming home and seeing me dead would have done to her. At that moment I realized how selfish I was. I was appalled at myself for thinking of committing such an act against someone I loved so deeply.

I quickly replaced the gun and jumped in bed.

"Are you sick?" I heard her say through my door. I replied with, "Yes," and she said she was too. Must have been my cooking. I laid in the dark for the rest of the day and night realizing suicide wasn't the answer, but what was?

I HAD CONVINCED MYSELF

that anyone who would willingly kill a child didn't deserve to live. Someone of my caliber was worthless. So I became even more rampant, to the point of being obsessed with death. I started a kind of "experiment" to see how many ways I could meet my demise: How much drugs and in what amount? How fast could my car really go? How many strangers could I meet before the wrong one picked me up? I didn't care how I lived any more because death was my mission.

I entered one romantic relationship after another without committing anything to anybody. Commitment meant that life would continue, and since my life needed to end, why bother? I found the perfect set up.

My favorite bar had a different live band each week. The joke around the bar was which guy from the new band would become my boyfriend for that week. The weirder the better. When we had a repeat band, I already knew who I would be with for that week. When that game didn't satisfy me anymore, I started spending all my extra money on concert tickets so that my girlfriend and I could not only get into the concert, but also get backstage to party with the band. On more than one occasion the band would send their roadies to come and get us out of the crowd and bring us backstage before the show. I realize now their invitation resulted from seeing us in tasteless, immodest attire. Of course, at the time, I took their actions as a compliment. Oddly enough, through all this partying sex was never an issue. My girlfriends and I kept our activities with these bands to strictly partying.

During those two years, I estimate that I attended around 100 concerts, and I partied with some of the greats from the 80's! Wow. I'm sure at one point in my life, I saw that as an achievement. Also during this time, I met a man that caught my eye.

He was the road manager for one of the more popular

bands from that era. He managed several different per-
formers, so the various concerts brought him to town
more often. While he was gone, we even wrote each other
a few times. I kind of liked this guy and was surprised at
myself for actually feeling something for him. All we had
done together was spend a few hours drinking and doing
drugs at the after concert parties.

One time he called to let me know he was going to be
in town alone and wanted to take me out. He asked me
to stop by his hotel and we would go out from there. He
was staying at the nicest hotel in town the one where the
concert parties would end up. When I arrived, I called
him from the lobby and he said he wasn't ready yet and
that I could come up to his room and talk to him while
he finished getting ready. I hardly knew him, but thought
nothing of going to his hotel room. He was in a suite that
overlooked the skyline of the city. It was a beautiful room
in which I felt out of place because I wasn't used to having
nice things like that around me. I had not been there long
when he began to make it clear why he wanted me there.

I was astonished, so I tried to leave the room, but he
wouldn't let me. He shoved me down on the bed and pinned
me down. He started pulling at my pants and I was holding
on to them for dear life. He even ripped them to get them off.
I fought with all I had, but he was the stronger one. I
finally gave up and lay helplessly while he raped me.

When he was through, he got off the bed and finished
getting ready. I went to the bathroom and saw I was bleed-
ing. I cleaned myself up and was able to get my pants back
together. I pulled my sweater down over the ripped part
and walked back into the hotel room like nothing had
happened. He then took me to a nice restaurant. The only

thing I remember from that night is that he paid for our meal with a Platinum American Express card, the first one I had ever seen. "Wow, he must be rich," I thought. A rich rapist. I knew somehow that I deserved what had just happened to me, that my past choices led to my present situation. There was no reason to tell anyone about the rape because I felt I deserved it anyway after all I had done.

I received a few more cards and phone calls from him after that night, but I didn't return them. Every time I thought of him I felt queasy. That night I got on my knees and asked God to get me out of this lifestyle. I told him I couldn't live like this any longer. I begged and pleaded with Him to show me a way out. The words he dropped into my mind are forever etched in my memory. "I'll have to handicap you to do it."

I immediately pictured myself in a wheelchair. I got up from my knees, and said, "No thank you. I'll figure my own way out."

I FELT LIKE A SHELL.

Just an empty version of my former self. When could I die? Did I have to keep waking up? When would these nightmares end? Why did I make this choice? The guilt was consuming me. Why would the image of my boyfriend on his knees, on my front porch crying uncontrollably not go away? How could I have just driven away from Brian's wishes? How could something this controlling and painful be legal? How could our society allow this to happen? Why didn't the sound of that machine dull with time? Was I being over-emotional? The media version of abortion contrasted so drastically from my personal experience, I even questioned my own sanity.

I knew that what the public was telling me was not the truth. What I was going through on the inside conflicted with what they were saying was an okay law in our books. Why didn't someone tell me? God, please forgive me. Yes, that may be the answer! I had learned as a child that I could ask forgiveness for sin and God would forgive me. So my daily mantra was, "God, forgive me. God, please forgive me. God would you please forgive me?" But I didn't feel forgiven.

So, the wild nights, the concerts, and the drunken parties continued. One night I was out with some of my girlfriends at a bar. The only thing I remember from that night was that I danced with someone and my friends told me he really liked me. In fact, he called me the next day. I didn't talk to him because I didn't even remember his face. He called again and asked me out. I said "Yes," because I didn't have any money and knew I would be able to get a good meal. Jack met me at my place and I was surprised to see that unlike my array of band members, he was dressed nice. He was very cute and drove a nice car. I found out he was from a good family and had a steady job. Wow. What did he want with me? I knew he drank excessively, but I went out with him and had a satisfying meal and a good time. He took me home and didn't even ask to come in. He didn't offer me drugs all night either. Wow again.

What was up with this guy? He was not the typical guy I dated-he almost seemed to respect me, to be too good for me, so I decided I wouldn't go out with him anymore, I wouldn't want to embarrass myself when he realized that I wasn't worthy of him.

Jack kept calling. I kept saying no. One year passed and he called again. I needed a meal, so I said, "Yes". The next day he sent a dozen red roses to my workplace. My friends were so jealous. I loved the attention. I went out with him a few more times and then reminded myself of my decision to avoid humiliation. So when he kept asking, I kept declining.

Months had passed since I asked God to show me a way out. All I could do was envision myself in a wheelchair. I merely existed day to day. The minute my mind would replay that horrid day and retrieve that image of my dreadful choice, I would either take a pill, smoke a joint, or drink a shot. I felt as though the earth was just stuck with me until I died. God, please forgive me.

I finally reached the point that life in a wheelchair seemed better to me than the life I was currently living. I got on my knees again and said, "Okay, God. Handicap me."

Jack called again. This time, I said, "Yes."

After this date, he sent another dozen red roses to my work. My friends were definitely jealous now and were telling me how crazy I was for not marrying this guy. But I knew it was just a matter of time before he would bolt and never come back. Then I missed my period.

OH GOD, PLEASE FORGIVE ME.

Please don't let me be in the same predicament. Oh God, I'll do anything. Please don't let me be pregnant.

I worked in an outpatient center that housed a lab onsite. I told my best friend at work my news, and she said to go immediately and find out the results. I walked into the lab, closed the door, and sat down. The lab technician, who was also my friend, asked what was wrong and said that I looked terrible. I told her I needed for her to draw some blood and test it for pregnancy. She did that immediately. She told me to go back to work and not to worry, and that she would call me in just a little while and calm my fears. I went back to my desk and tried to concentrate until I heard the buzz on my phone. It was my friend who said, "Sheila, I think you need to come back here." I walked, but didn't know if I was going to fall down or just pass out.

She stood in the lab with the test in her hand and a grave look on her face. I took the test and started to cry. The first words out of my mouth were, "I'll never live through another abortion." She looked startled and I realized I just let out my most guarded secret. She told me that she didn't know what I was going to do, but that I needed to get back to work and that everything would be okay.

I went back to my desk and the somber look on my face told my friend everything she needed to know. She was pregnant at the time, just barely showing. I told her of my abortion and how I knew there was no way I would ever live through another one. She took my hands, looked me in the eyes, and said, "We'll get through this together. We'll be pregnant together--won't that be fun?" Now "fun" was not the word I would have chosen at that moment to describe my feelings, but I knew she was trying to encourage me. I needed a true friend at that moment and she was it. She didn't reject me when she found out about my abortion and that resonated deeply within me. She was the first person I had told that didn't reject me.

How did I end up in this situation again? God, please forgive me. I was just disgusted with myself. My life was so messed up. Abortion was not even an option, so what was I going to do? I was 22. My life had gone off the deep end in just three short years. Praying to God evidently didn't change anything. In fact, it was worse. Now I was going to be pregnant and in a wheelchair. How would I take care of a child when I was confined to a wheelchair?

I denied my pregnancy for a long time. I didn't speak of it again to my friend at work and I didn't tell anyone else. I decided I would make myself have a miscarriage. That way it wouldn't be an abortion and it would offer me a way out of this situation.

So, for the next four months, I did everything in my power to miscarry my child. I volunteered to help a girl at work move. I lifted and carried the heaviest boxes. I moved couches, chairs, and tables, anything that required more strength than I had. I went home that day so sore and tired. She sure did appreciate all my hard work! Nevertheless, I was still pregnant.

I moved office furniture and I drank like a fish, but

I didn't take any more drugs. I don't really know why. I guess it was my subconscious jolting into action. I lost weight steadily. I didn't go to the doctor. I was slowly destroying myself.

I never mentioned my pregnancy to my friend again, but she watched me in silence. Little did I know she was faithfully praying.

ONE DAY MY FRIENDS

at the outpatient center wanted to test their new ultrasound equipment so they thought I would be the perfect candidate. We whisked away to the ultrasound room and started testing. My purpose was to ensure the equipment worked, but I was not at all prepared for what happened. As I lay down, I looked at the ultrasound monitor, and I saw him. All of him. I saw his entire body: his developing brain, tiny legs, little arms, and beating heart. My eyes instantly flooded with tears that ran down both cheeks. My two friends looked at me so sweetly as they would have a new mom seeing her precious son for the first time. What they didn't realize was that the tears did not flow out of a joyful heart, but from a shameful one. I had just witnessed my perfectly formed baby, but the realization that he was alive made me cry in pain for my first child. The one whose life I felt justified by the Supreme Court to end. The baby that was meant to be here but was not because it wasn't "right" for me and my body. What I was seeing was a real baby that was depending on me to keep his blood flowing, his brain forming, and his heart beating. He depended on my life to sustain his.

No, I could not enjoy that precious moment because it was stolen from me under the guise of choice. Instead, that moment showed to me the consequence I had to endure, knowing that I paid someone 250 bucks to end the life that grew inside me. How could I have ever done this? God, please forgive me.

IT WAS NOW NEW YEARS EVE.

I was at my favorite bar with the weekly live bands. I was four months pregnant and still denying anything was wrong in my life. I still wore my jeans comfortably, my pregnancy not evident at all. But after midnight, something happened. I felt like someone slapped me across the face. I jumped down off the chair in which I was dancing, realizing I was suddenly completely sober, when just seconds before I had been wasted. I sat down and God said to me so plainly in words I will never forget: "You can continue on with this lifestyle and give birth to a retarded child, or you can straighten up your act and give birth to a healthy one. It's your choice."

I was now handicapped. God had handicapped me and I didn't even realize it. He had given me exactly what

I asked for: This pregnancy was my handicap to wake me up and slow me down. God, please forgive me. I made my girlfriend leave immediately. I drove us. I was stone sober.

The next day I lay on my couch in stunned silence watching the day's onslaught of football games. The realization of the fact that I was truly going to have a baby in five short months was sinking in. The phone rang. It was Jack. He said he just wanted to call and tell me Happy New Year. I knew I was going to have to tell him I was pregnant eventually. Oh, I didn't want to. He asked me out for later in the month, and I said, "Yes."

I called my sister, Kim, the next day and told her I was pregnant. She cried and then she got excited. How could she be excited? I asked her for the name and phone number of her midwife, and then I called and made my first appointment. The next day I came home and my kitchen was filled with groceries. My sister had left me a note saying that if I was going to be giving birth to her niece or nephew she wanted to make sure I was eating healthy. She just gave me what I had been missing all along: support. I had kept people at a distance. I rejected them before they had a chance to reject me. My sister kept the pregnancy a secret from the rest of our family. I wasn't quite ready to tell everyone. The pressures I would face being unmarried, having no money, and planning to raise a child by myself were enough to dwell on for right now.

I went to the midwife, started taking vitamins, and began taking care of myself. I didn't have another drink through the rest of my pregnancy.

Later that month, my belly suddenly started to grow! Therefore, some of my clothes were getting too small and my growing belly was getting harder and harder to hide. When Jack called to confirm that we were still going out, I knew I had to tell him before he showed up at my door and met my belly first. He probably wouldn't want to continue with our relationship after he knew, anyway. He tried several times to get off the phone. Finally, I ran out of conversation starters.

I said, "Before we hang up, I have something to tell you."

He said, "Okay."

I said, "I'm pregnant."

I was already guarded and had a speech ready if he suggested abortion. I knew that I was going to tell him to get out of my life and never call me back. The very idea so disgusted me.

All he said was, "I know."

I said, "Okay," and then hung up the phone as quickly as I could.

How did he know? Who had told him? What was he thinking? He knew I was pregnant and didn't mention abortion? What are his motives? Is he going to wait until we see each other to suggest abortion?

January 23, 1988, the day of our scheduled date, I had transitioned into maternity clothes. It was amazing to me how fast my belly grew. When he picked me up, we both acted like we didn't notice the big fat belly. I grabbed my coat, and we and my big fat belly headed out the door. I put my seatbelt around my big fat belly and me. (Oh, dear God, I'm dying here.) He drove us to a nice restaurant where we were seated. Thank God, finally a table where I can hide my big fat belly. The service was so slow, it took an eternity to get our food. But that long wait gave us time

and forced us to divulge more and more about our situation and ourselves.

He told me that the very reason he had called me on
New Years Day was because he had been at a party the
night before and had heard I was pregnant. I guess the
word was getting around. We talked briefly about the
future without committing too much of ourselves to it.
Both of us were very cautious not to reveal too much of
our feelings or ourselves. One thing he was sure to tell
me was how proud he was that I didn't choose abortion.
He told me that his personal feelings were that abortion
would be a terrible thing for any woman to choose. He
praised me for making the right decision. If he only knew.
My safeguarded secret just got locked away for good without a remote chance of escaping.

He drove me home and we made plans to watch the
Super Bowl together. The next day I received two dozen
red roses at work. Oh my goodness. You can imagine
the excitement of my co-workers as they told me that I
shouldn't let him get away. After all, he was a normal, and
even romantic, guy.

But when it was time for our Super Bowl date, he
called me and told me he was sick. I took his cancellation
of our date as total rejection. All those old, negative, self-
destructive feelings came flooding back. I was worthless.
What would ever make me think I could get and keep a
guy this good? I was crazy to let my guard down. Now I
was humiliated again. I called my girlfriend and we got
together for the Super Bowl and bashed him all night long.
He was a 'typical' man. I should have known it from the
start.

AFTER SEVERAL DAYS PASSED,

he called and I was very short with him. I was not going to let him reject me before I rejected him. He overlooked my curt remarks and proceeded to tell me how he almost ended up in the hospital because he had been so sick. He had been vomiting for days, and was so dehydrated that he had missed work. At that point, he didn't even know who had won the Super Bowl. I meekly told him it was Washington.

I still was so unsure. Do I proceed to let a decent man come into my life? What was this new feeling I was having in my heart? There was something there that I had not felt in a very long time. But what was it? Love? No. God, forgive me for March 29. I don't deserve goodness in my life.

He asked me to go out with him again for Valentine's Day. By this time I had told my entire family of my pregnancy. Each person had his own opinion--abortion, adoption. There was no way a nervous, broken, damaged 22-year old girl should even introduce a child into this world. It would make absolutely no sense considering my past. So I totally understood why my family was offering alternatives. However, alternatives were not an option in my mind, so I would go forward with this pregnancy and make the most of my situation.

On Valentine's Day he showed up with dinner. We

were sitting in my kitchen eating and he said he had a little gift for me, so he left to go get it from the car. I thought he would return with another dozen roses, but instead, he entered my apartment with a wheel in his hands. When I saw that precious wheel, I knew I was in love with him. Yes, it may seem to be a pretty bizarre Valentine's Day gift, but let me explain its significance.

I had been driving a little Mazda for more than a year with a bent wheel. My car shook so violently as I drove, people would pull up beside me to let me know I had a bent wheel. After I would get out of my car, for thirty minutes I would feel as though I had been operating a jackhammer. I lived with the vibration because I had no money to fix it. I spent all my money on car payments and credit cards. So for him to walk through the door carrying a wheel was profound statement of concern and care for my well being.

Oh God, please forgive me. I don't deserve this. Do I dare let myself feel this way? Do I dare let him see that I love him? He wanted to take care of our child and me. Not one man had ever seemed to value me the way Jack did. No one had ever cared for me to this extent. But why? I was so worthless. Why and how could anyone love me the way he seems to?

He would never find out my secret. I know all of the roses and romance would be over in the blink of an eye if he ever found out.

DURING THIS TIME

my other sister and her husband had allowed me to come and live with them to help me get some of my credit cards paid off. My sisters really rallied around me during this extremely tough time in my life and I will forever be grateful for their support.

I was able to relax, work, and save as much money as possible for the couple of months I lived with her. I was also able to focus more on Jack and our developing relationship.

The next week, he surprised me at work and had prepared a big picnic lunch. As we settled in at the park to have the picnic, he began to unload his basket. First he unpacked the food, then-what was that? Baby clothes made for a boy! Tiny little shoes! Little bitty blue outfits! Our son's first baby clothes were being shown one by one by a man that cared for me. And now I knew he cared for our son, soon to be born in a few short weeks.

We sat together at the park that day and cried. There were tears of joy, fear, and uncertainty. I loved him. I really loved him.

MY DUE DATE OF MAY 21

came and went. But on May 26, I felt the first twinge of pain as we sat together watching a movie. I wasn't sure, but maybe it was time. He grabbed his clipboard and stopwatch and began the timing he had learned in our Lamaze classes. He had come prepared.

Sure enough, five minutes later I felt another sensation. Could it be? I was so anxious and scared! Five minutes later, another one happened. This pattern continued for hours. We called my midwife, excited and nervous. She told us to calm down and to head to the hospital when they started coming quicker. Well, "quicker" didn't happen--they were five minutes apart the entire night. We were exhausted. When we went to her office the next day, "quicker" came after she broke my water.

I had invited most of my family, Jack's family, and just about all my friends into the labor and delivery room with me. There were a total of 13 people in the room when Jarod was born on May 27, 1988. When he was handed to me, what should have been one of the most joyous moments of my life was instead flooded with guilt. Why couldn't I have made this same choice for my first child? How did I deserve this perfectly healthy, beautiful child?

I just knew that everyone who was standing around the bed looking at Jack and me and our precious child were all wondering, "Are they ever going to get married?" I was wondering how I was ever going to function normally and keep my secret. I couldn't get too attached to our son because I knew God would take him from me to make me pay for that dreaded day back in 1985. I looked at him and cried. How I longed to love him. How I longed to be the mother he needed. But I knew I never could be.

JACK HAD FOUND me a nicer apartment that I could afford in a better part of town. On the first night in the apartment when everyone left and it was just the three of us, we looked at each other and I could see the fear in Jack's eyes. He said that he was afraid that since I had my own apartment and the baby was born that I wouldn't need him any longer. Quite the opposite was true. I was terrified he would leave me.

We didn't officially move in together, but we were never apart except the hours he worked. I knew that my lack of emotion kept him at arms length. I worked so hard to keep my secret. After all, he thought I was great for not choosing abortion. I could never let him find out the truth about me.

I got to know Jarod intimately the weeks I was home recuperating. He was the most beloved person I had ever known. I never knew that a love like that existed between two people. It was so easy to love! I realized through those weeks that what I perceived as a handicap was not a handicap at all. God had given me one of the greatest, most precious, fragile gifts I had ever received to save my life from destruction. This child was a true gift from God. I knew this child had a special purpose and plan and it was my job to help him find that purpose and pursue it. I felt so honored to be his mother and still feel that way today. But always there was that nagging, continuing feeling of emptiness that somehow this was not going to last. This child was going to be taken away from me. I was somehow going to be punished for that choice I made, and that punishment was going to be never being able to see my son again.

Several weeks later, Jack came home from work, got down on one knee, opened up a little black velvet box, and asked me to marry him. Of course I said, "Yes."

We were married August 6, 1988. We had a huge wedding. Jarod wore a white tux, just as Jack wore, and was in all the wedding pictures. It was a very happy day for me. I thought, "Finally, I'm going to be happy. This crazy life I have been living is over. I can put it all behind me. He'll never know my secret, and we can get on with our life together, the three of us."

WE WERE BOTH SO EXCITED

to start our new life together. I had never been so elated. I had never had a real family; so to have a family meant the entire world to me. As a young girl I never would allow my mind to think of being married, having a nice home full of children, things that most girls dream about. Those thoughts seemed so far beyond anything that would or could happen to me, so why waste time imagining?

In 1970, when I was four years old, my mother was driving us home through a rainstorm. She lost control of the car. I was thrown through the windshield, and she was killed instantly. She was everything to me, and in one minute, everything was gone. My sisters and I spent the next six years of our lives living either with our father, or with different neighbors. My father loved us, but was unable to be a caretaker after losing his 29-year-old wife. However, my aunt and uncle were equipped to handle a family, so they stepped in and took us. I will forever be grateful for their sacrifice.

Those five years I lived with my aunt and uncle were the most precious of my childhood. My uncle is with Jesus now, but before he moved on to eternity I was able to tell him what his sacrifice meant to me. I will forever cherish that conversation. Because of their example, I will eternally be an advocate for adoption. Adoption is the chance to give children a life that otherwise they wouldn't have. That is what my father, my aunt, and my uncle did for me. It changed my life for the better and will continue to bless generations after me.

So to have a family where I could create stability and raise Jarod in a completely different environment was an awesome opportunity. When I focused just on that I would be fine. But then when the other thoughts would creep in... that was another story.

I WANTED TO BELIEVE

that this fairy tale would last, but I felt God was going to make me pay for that one choice I made back in 1985. I knew the only way He could do that was to take my son or my husband from me. A life for a life, isn't that what the Bible says? I knew God held fast and true to His word and I knew His word to be 100% absolutely truthful, so I waited, I drank, and I waited some more.

If Jack was five minutes late, I would start standing by the window watching and waiting to see if he was really going to come home. What if he had left me, or was dead in a ditch somewhere? If he was ten minutes late, I would get on the phone with his work and find out exactly what time he left and I would calculate exactly when he should be pulling in the driveway. On more than one occasion, I had put Jarod in to the car and driven the route home he would have taken so I could find him. What if there had been a horrific car crash? Jack would find out about my paranoia and would become furious with me for tailing him because of a small ten minutes. I know I was driving him absolutely crazy with my worry.

I would be up three to four times per night to listen to the monitor to make sure I could still hear Jarod breathing. If I couldn't I would race frantically into the nursery and put my finger under his nose to make sure breath was still coming out. I was trying to outsmart God. I think subconsciously I was going to protect my family by doing all these crazy things. That way, I could stay one step ahead of God and be the one in control. I was the one who was going to keep God from taking my two loves from me.

This behavior was driving me mad, it was driving my husband mad, and my son had no hope of turning out normal with a mother like me. I was trying so hard, but yet failing miserably. I wanted to be happy, but knew I didn't deserve to be. The minute I would start having a good time and be happy, the memories would surface. Then the thoughts would start, so I would drink to forget.

The reality of my situation was that I was married and had a family, which was a thought beyond my wildest dreams. I had a horrible secret from my husband that I knew would end this entire love affair if only he knew. In the meantime I was waiting for God to reveal how He was going to make me pay for the child I aborted. So I drank. I drank a lot. I would start in the late afternoon, so by the time I was sloshed, Jack would be home to take care of Jarod.

God, I beg you to forgive me. I know I'm not forgiven. Why won't you forgive me? Why must I continue on this way? Where is the relief? How am I going to continue keeping this secret from Jack?

LESS THAN A YEAR

after we were married I was pregnant again. It was a wonderful occasion! We told our family and I could tell they were glad we did it in the right order this time. I was genuinely happy, too. I couldn't wait to have what I hoped was another little boy. I really wanted two boys that would be close in age, grow up together and share clothes and a room, and play with their dog in a big yard. I could imagine how perfect it would be. I had it all under control.

The pregnancy was tough--it seemed as though something was always wrong with me. I never forgot those words God spoke to me on that fateful New Years Eve night, so I didn't drink during the pregnancy. The doctor set my due date for March 26. Wow, that was awfully close to March 29. For years I had put a big star on my calendar and reminded myself to hate myself two weeks before and at least two weeks after. I needed to punish my very existence by reliving every sordid detail so I would never forget this shameful choice I had made.

As this pregnancy progressed, my mind would not let me forget my secret. I couldn't turn to alcohol to fix it, so I tried to deal with it on my own. It was unmanageable, so a few months into the pregnancy; I was ready to tell Jack my most regretful secret. I foresaw that he was going to leave me. All of this would be over. This is how God would make me pay. He would use my choice to turn my own husband against me. One morning I woke up and knew it was the day of truth. I waited until he got home from work, prepared dinner, put Jarod to bed, sat down, and told him I had to talk to him.

ALL DAY LONG

I had thought about the times he repeatedly told me how proud he was of me for not choosing abortion for Jarod. God, please forgive me. Why are you making me do this?

As I began to tell him, I was sobbing uncontrollably. He cried without even knowing what was wrong. It upset him terribly to see me like this. As the words came tumbling out I knew in my mind I was ending my marriage. I had pictured him fighting me for custody of Jarod, knowing someone like me should never deserve to parent another child. As I talked he cried harder and so did I. I couldn't believe what was happening. God, please forgive me. Why do I have to burden this good man with my horrid past? Why must he live with this too? But then something happened. He wrapped his arms around me and through his tears said, "We'll get through this. We'll find you help. I love you." Without even knowing it, he represented the love of Christ to me in an unfathomable way. I didn't know that then and neither did he, but I certainly know it now.

I looked at him and couldn't believe what I was hearing. He's staying? He loves me? I don't disgust him? But what about all those times he said how proud he was of me? He assured me that didn't change. He was still proud of me. Nothing before that mattered. I was still the same person he fell in love with. Could I be hearing what I think I'm hearing?

The next several days I walked on eggshells. Is he going to come home? Am I going to come home to an empty apartment and a farewell letter? Is all of this too good to be true?

We came to the end of the pregnancy and both of us looked forward with great anticipation to meet our little boy. March 26 came and went with no signs of my son being in a hurry to get out. On March 28 I felt that familiar twinge. We went through the labor as the day wore on. Apparently he wanted to stay where he was. I was so tired, so Jack was by my side to help me breathe during each contraction.

Jakob finally decided to come out at 4:30 a.m. on March 29. Ten other people helped me bring this precious child into the world, but not one of them except Jack knew the significance of that day. As soon as Jakob was born, my husband leaned over to my ear and whispered, "Now instead of a day of mourning, God has given us a day of celebration!" Oh, I was on Cloud Nine! I knew God had forgiven me. I knew this had to be over. Thank you, God, for forgiving me. Why in the world would you give me such a gift on the very day I destroyed one of yours?

Believe it or not I came home from the hospital that afternoon. I was ready to get on with life. I had a new outlook. I knew this nightmare was over. We were going to make it after all.

When we arrived home, we snapped so many pictures and had so many family members at our house, we just had a celebration party for a few days. Life was good. I was ready to recuperate and start raising my two boys.

Finally the company slowed, Jack went back to work and there I was left alone with my two boys, and my thoughts. Those thoughts. But they were supposed to be gone! I had them under control! Everything was going great! What happened? So back to the tequila I went.

TEQUILA BECAME MY COMPANION.

I found every way imaginable to make margaritas. I made them with every kind of fruit, shaken, stirred, on the rocks, frozen, with sugar, and with salt. You name it; I've probably drank it. Drinking was my favorite hobby.

I used the liquor once again to get my mind off my problems. Why could I not get my head cleared? My husband didn't leave me when I told him of my abortion, I felt like God had finally forgiven me--He had even given me another child on the very day I had an abortion. But what was still wrong with me? Why did I still continue to fail miserably as a wife and a mother? It was so important to me to make sure my family was protected--that this haven I had created was forever untouched by the person I once was. I didn't want anything from my past to enter this cherished area of my life. But yet I couldn't keep my decision away. It was constantly haunting me, forever in my thoughts.

I knew my drinking was out of control. I drank every day. I wanted to stop, so I told myself to drink only on the weekends. Then every day something would happen to justify why I should take a drink. Then after failing at that I would say I wasn't going to have a drink except on Tuesday, Thursday, and the weekends. Then after failing at that I would say, I'm not going to drink except until after 6:00 p.m. every day, and at that I would fail too.

It was the only thing I could do that would guarantee a good night's sleep. Sleep was what I needed to get away from the nightmares and away from the sound of that machine they used on me. It was the only thing that would calm my nerves, so I used this reason to justify being a drunk in front of my kids and everyone I knew.

All our friends were heavy drinkers as well. We associated with people who didn't make us feel guilty for our wrong lifestyle. We loved these people and did everything with them. We went on vacations together, celebrated birthdays together, spent every weekend together, and they were our whole life. Every activity centered on drinking. It was perfect.

To ease my guilty conscience from drinking so much and to try to pay my penance for what I had done, I would drag my family to church on occasion. My husband had no interest in church, but went to appease me. I think I had convinced him that the boys needed to be in church. Of course they didn't leave my side. I refused to put my children in the church nursery for fear that something might happen to them. I had to be in total control of their well being. Remember, I had to be one step ahead of God.

So a few times a year, we would attend church unknowingly on the day the local pregnancy resource center showed up to speak and receive an offering. I hated that day. The speaker would talk of how horrible abortion is, but I could not hear them offering me any hope whatsoever. As soon as they stated where they were from and they began talking about the travesty of abortion, I would begin to have a physical reaction. My blood pressure would rise, my face would turn red, I would start to cry, and then I would sweat from head to toe. What I wanted to do was go running and screaming out the back door never to return. But I knew if I moved an inch, people would notice and I would instantly be branded as one of those disgusting people who have had an abortion.

One thing I knew for sure, there was no way I was going to turn to my church for help. They made it clear how they stood on abortion, and never answered my two questions: Can I turn back to God? Is it too late for me? So I continued to ride my roller coaster of emotions.

MY HUSBAND NEVER KNEW

who he was going to come home to: Happy Sheila, Crying Sheila, Drunk Sheila, or Mad Sheila. On some days, I was in control of my emotions--I was going to put everything behind me and keep moving forward. The next day I would wake up from a nightmare and I would dread hav-

ing to face another day of being reminded of killing my
first child. I felt guilty every day as I looked at my precious boys' faces that gave me such happiness, love, and
joy, knowing I did not deserve one ounce of the love they
shared.

I had suicidal thoughts on a weekly basis. I knew they
would be better off being raised by someone else and not
someone crazy like me. The only thing that kept me from
going through with suicide was the memory of my stepsister pulling into the driveway and then imagining what the
people left behind go through. I didn't want to put Jack,
or the boys through that. But yet, what was the answer?
How would I ever be released from this mental prison I
put myself in?

One day I was driving down the road with the boys. I
had the radio tuned to a Christian radio station. A com-
mercial came on the air from the local pregnancy resource
center. They were advertising a class they were about to
teach that was for "women who were suffering after the
choice of abortion." My jaw dropped and I looked at the
radio dial to make sure I was hearing what I thought I was
hearing. I turned up the volume to hear more. They gave
the phone number and the location. I couldn't believe it.
It was one of the greatest discoveries of my life. I felt like
someone who had just won the lottery. There were others. There were really others. If they had to actually form
a class to help people like me, then how many others are
there? There can't be many as emotionally unstable as I
was...maybe 10 or 12.

My mind was racing. It was 1992, before anyone
had cell phones. I went immediately home and called the
number. The person I spoke with on the phone told me

where to go for the class and what time it started. I was so
excited. I couldn't collect all my thoughts. Maybe I'll have
a drink and think about all of this.

So could it be possible that I'm not crazy after all?
Could it be that other people are feeling the same way?
Surely so, if they had to actually form a class. This is
just too good to be true. Yes, it was too good to be true.
Those people will see me as trash. I am trash. Why would
they want to help me? What do they really want? What if
I know someone? What was I thinking? They're the ones
that come to my church and speak. People from my church
probably work there. If I go to this class they'll see me and
know the truth about me. Well forget that. What a stupid
idea.

The night of the meeting I decided to go drinking with
my girlfriends, all the while looking at my watch wondering if I should have gone to that "stupid" class.

I waited a week or two and called them back. I set
another appointment and then allowed the thoughts to
come back of how gullible I was, thinking there was real
help for me. Again, I didn't go. I cancelled two more times
after that, and then I called back. I couldn't believe the
women at the center would even take my phone calls after
four missed appointments, but they did.

The receptionist told me a new class was starting and
let me know all the details. I finally gained enough courage to go to a meeting. I met two other women there who
looked like I felt. They were terrified and on the verge of
tears. On my turn to talk, I told them my entire story. I
couldn't believe the words were coming out of me. I was
really telling total strangers my deepest, darkest secret. I
thought I was really crazy for doing this. But what amazed

me was these two other women were telling my story too. They had the same war in their mind that I was having. How could this be? I was astounded that I had spent the past seven years feeling so alone, yet there were these two other women in my same town who were feeling the exact same way. I knew I was making yet another discovery I would always remember. I left the class that day feeling like I had made one of the smartest decisions I had made in a long time.

WEEKS PASSED

and I could feel my head getting clearer. I was talking to God more, so I was filling it up with Him. I could almost feel the wound healing. How could this be? I felt good. I felt normal again.

Through this class I was able to pinpoint my problem. I had not been able to forgive myself. I knew and believed God had forgiven me, I learned that in my youth group. But what had driven me so crazy is why I was still so messed up. What about forgiveness is so hard to accept? Why was I unable to forgive myself?

I never missed a single class. For twelve weeks I drove to the other side of town to spend two hours talking and dealing with a subject I had worked harder at than anything in my life to keep secret. Now I was talking about it every week to total strangers.

They didn't remain strangers for very long. They became my life raft. These two incredibly brave women became my bridge back to the one true source that could free me and totally heal me. The Ultimate Healer...Jesus Christ. Wow, what a revelation. I didn't know how it was happening, but I could tell something supernatural was taking place in my mind and my heart. I was waking up happy and was able to remain happy throughout the day. Sure I had some down days just like everyone else, but I was able to handle them. They didn't send me over the edge into a drunken stupor any more. I didn't need the alcohol as a crutch any longer because I was starting to face each day with a different attitude. It was not me battling the thoughts, but me just living another day.

Every week was an experiment to see if the Bible study really worked. Not until around week 10 did I begin to embrace it with my entire being. I really was getting well. My mind really was healing. This gaping wound really was closing. This really was happening to me and I couldn't have been more astonished, more overjoyed, and more thankful.

The women who had become my bridge back to God taught me I could now approach Him on my own. The God of my youth who had been waiting patiently by my side all these years was now so ever present in my life. I don't have words to write on this page how thankful I was He never left me, even when I felt He had.

The last two weeks of the class we focused on our children, that is, our aborted children. I was glad I had gone through ten weeks of intense healing before completing this exercise. It was one of the most difficult things I've ever had to do. I had to pray and in my mind face my child and the reality of the choice I made to end her life.

I had to finally recognize her as a part of my life and a part of my family. I was at last allowed to bestow on her the dignity and worth she never received. I ended her life so unnaturally and abruptly. Now I was able to reach into my past and right this wrong as much as I possibly could as a human. My supernatural God did the rest.

I can honestly say I graduated from the Bible study with so much relief flooding through me. Finally I was able to lay down this burden and pick up a new life. God had flowed through me to reach me, to change my mind about just how far His grace extends and I was able to move forward with a new outlook.

Immediately after graduating from the Bible study I felt so good and I wanted this feeling to be permanent. The next week I signed up at the local pregnancy center in Chattanooga, TN to learn how to teach that same Bible study. I wanted to see other women find the freedom that I had found.

I received my training over the next several weeks and was turned loose to start teaching the class. I was so excited. I started out being the co-facilitator so I could continue to learn about different women's situations and responses. I was amazed at the number of courageous women that would come forward every time we offered a class.

I couldn't help but remember and laugh at my thinking there would just be five or six total women who needed help. However, five or six women were in every class we offered, and people were even waiting for another class to start.

I loved my time in those abortion recovery classes when the light bulb would turn on in the minds of the women.

You could see that moment in their eyes. I anticipated the moment when they realized that they could be forgiven for having an abortion, and that they could forgive themselves as well. I often describe it as being better than front and center on Broadway, or the 50-yard line at the Super Bowl.

One thing I vividly remember during my time teaching these classes is a phrase that I heard repeatedly. The phrase went like this: "If I could just save one unborn baby, I would tell my story." Knowing from first hand experience how hard it is to tell an abortion story, I always paid close attention. I respected and admired the woman who would say that phrase. I didn't know if I even had enough guts to tell my story in public. It was a safe environment in the confines of the Bible study. But to go out in plain view, well that was something that I just had not let my mind even think about.

Would I tell my abortion story if it saved only one unborn baby? Would I be willing to risk ridicule and judgment for the life of one baby? Am I willing to go that far to protect the innocent lives of both the child and the mother? What exactly am I willing to do? These were all questions that needed answers but I wasn't sure I was ready to give them. So I stuffed those nagging questions in the back of my mind and continued to assist in the comfortable surroundings of the class.

The pregnancy center was located directly across the street from the abortion clinic in which I had my abortion. I felt a sense of vengeance every time I pulled on to the pregnancy center's parking lot, knowing I was doing all I knew to do to combat what was going on across the street.

ONE DAY

my husband received news that his company wanted to transfer him to Nashville, TN. Because of all the bad memories I would be leaving behind in Chattanooga, I couldn't get my family packed quickly enough.

Two months later when we pulled out behind the moving truck I kept waiting for the floodgate of emotions to open. After all, we were leaving my hometown. The gate never opened. I was happy to be leaving and I already loved Nashville.

I looked at this move as a new beginning; a new start to a new life with a new outlook. I was armed with a list of churches for us to visit. My husband was still not fully sold on the church idea, but knew it was best for the kids, so he obliged occasionally. I would stay out of church with him whenever he didn't "feel" like going. It just seemed easier than getting up and dressing our kids all by myself.

We visited a few churches and didn't like any of them. We moved in January and by April of 1994 we were going to the next church on the list; Cornerstone Church. After that first Sunday, we never visited another one. I knew we had found our home. My husband wasn't too sure about this being the "home" church, but he just went along with me so I would be happy. It was good for the kids after all.

I saw this new church as my fresh start. I wanted all

of these people we were meeting to not know the old Sheila. The one who went to every concert in town to get backstage; the one who had chosen abortion; the one who drank herself in to a stupor; and the list could go on. I wanted these people to only know the Sheila who had cleaned herself up. The one who went to church, who was raising her boys in church, who was all dressed up, ready to be in church. My husband played along and truly acted the part. He still drank every day as I did, but I had it under control-I really felt I could control my addiction.

A couple of years after we occasionally attended Cornerstone I became convicted of our lifestyle. I felt as though we were projecting one image at church, but then came home and drank and projected yet another image. What were we teaching our boys? I was unable to invite any of our church friends over because of all the alcohol in the house.

I started speaking out to Jack about it and he brushed me off with no regard. He didn't want to hear about my convictions. If I felt like I shouldn't be drinking then I needed to stop drinking and leave him alone. He continued to bring alcohol home every day and I would sometimes drink a whole bottle of wine every evening. But I had it under control. Really...I did...

I lived with these convictions for about two more years. I would try to stop drinking, but didn't have the will to stop. Then one day, my husband who had played the part as the loving Christian mate came home and announced to our family that on that day, September 6, 1998, he had been saved! Not only had he received his salvation but he also was delivered from wanting any kind of alcoholic drink whatsoever.

We spent that entire day pouring every last bottle of liquor, wine, and beer down the drain. We had huge garbage bags full of empty bottles. It was so much fun! We have not drunk together since that day, because it was then that I felt released from alcohol as well. Jack was a huge influence, and when he took a stand, I stood in agreement with him.

I WAS SO HAPPY when we went back to church. I finally felt like I was being who I was created to be-a real person with a purpose. I was ready to give my whole life, past, present, and future to God. I'll never forget that day being on the front row beside my husband. I had both hands raised in praise to God, totally abandoned to Him when I prayed, "God I'm ready for you to use me. Like Jack uses a hammer, use me as a tool in your hands."

To this day I warn people to be deeply conscious of what they pray for because shortly after I prayed that prayer was when the dreams started.

A huge crowd was watching me tell my story. This wasn't just a crowd either---this was thousands of people. I was on stage telling them all about my abortion. I was terrified, but it was as if an unstoppable force was inside me urging me on, making the right words come out of my mouth. I would shake myself until I woke up. I wanted off that stage and out from behind that podium, and wanted to be in a place that was comfortable.

God had set me free from a horrific choice I made years ago. I've paid my penance. Why is He reminding me now again, in a different form? I have a new life, free from that old, dead Sheila. Why is she being resurrected? Why am I reliving this?

These dreams went on for months to the point that Jack would put his hands on my head and pray that I could get a good night's sleep and not be awakened by the "nightmares."

One Sunday I was sitting in our church, which at the time had about one thousand members. I looked around the sanctuary and it was like every fourth woman shone like a beacon of light. They were everywhere. I knew that one out of every four women had had an abortion. I felt God speak to me at that moment and say, "I have given you this knowledge to help others and you're not doing anything with it." I knew what He was asking me to do.

I spent the next several weeks teetering, trying to work up the courage to call our Christian Education pastor and plan a meeting. Finally I complied and went to this meeting kicking and screaming the entire way. I knew I would be fine as long as I didn't have to tell our senior pastor. I could get through telling this one pastor, but no one else.

By now we had attended the church for five years and this man was a dear friend of ours. He thought it odd that I arranged a formal meeting with him when we hung out regularly on the weekends. I proceeded to tell him the entire story of my abortion, and what I felt God was asking me to do. After my talking for about thirty minutes, I was mentally drained. He had listened intently with tears in his eyes. As soon as I sat back exhausted and so happy it was over, he hit the button on his phone and buzzed our senior pastor into his office for me to tell him the same story. Oh my God, help me, why did I ever think I could do this!

So, off I went. I told him the entire story I had told not even five minutes before. After an hour of talking to both of them, they loved the idea and booked me to teach the first ever abortion recovery Bible study at Cornerstone Church.

You may be thinking that I walked out of the church elated. That was the very last thing I felt. I was kicking myself. I was thinking that maybe the dreams weren't that bad. After all, I could have ignored them until they went away. Why did I just bare my soul to these two men whom I respected and loved? What was I thinking? They probably think I'm trash. They're probably inside the office right now laughing at how stupid I was to make that choice. They'll probably change their minds after they've had time to think about it.

My mind was racing with these thoughts, none of them from God. But I allowed them in and did not even tell my closest friends that I was teaching this class. I figured I could coast under the radar and thought no one would ever show up for a class like this anyway. What was I thinking?

Coasting under the radar was my intention, but certainly not my pastor's intention. The week before the class started, he announced my plans to the entire church, and then proceeded to read a letter that a grieving mother had written to her aborted child. It was a letter filled with pain, sorrow, regret, and shame. That morning was one of the most touching, tender moments our church had experienced up to that point. In fact, people still comment on that letter today and remember when he read it I get tears in my eyes when I remember looking around me and seeing grown men and women weeping at the painful words they were hearing. My pastor couldn't even get through the letter without having to stop several times to gather himself.

After reading the letter, my pastor made me stand up in the middle of the sanctuary and wave my hand to the huge congregation so everyone would see the crazy lady who thinks she can teach the abortion recovery class. Okay, that might not have been his exact words, but that was what I heard. That was the first my friends had heard of my experience. Yes, I did the right thing. Thank you, God. Your ways are the best ways. You are so awesome.

I SAT ALONE

in the room of the church and waited on the women I hoped were coming. My mind started thinking hopelessly again. I thought that maybe no one would show up and I could put this whole crazy idea behind me. There would probably be no one here that even needs help like this. I knew that was a lie from satan, but for some reason I thought it anyway.

It came time for class to start. The room was still empty. I could hear crickets chirping in the background. I was embarrassed, kicking myself, asking myself again what made me do this. I heard all the classroom doors shut and knew the other rooms were filled with eager students. I was located on the busiest hallway at our church, so I knew that would probably hurt our attendance, but that's where they put me so I didn't protest. I knew God would have to work out the details. But still, no one? Was there really no one coming? I was so disappointed.

Then I saw a very reluctant face look at me through the window in the door. I motioned for her to come in. I was so happy someone showed up. Then immediately there was another, then another, until there were ten women sitting in the circle. I was grinning from ear to ear by this time, thanking God that He helped me overcome my reluctance and forced me to push forward with this class.

It was obvious these women simply waited until they felt no one would see them come into this class. They were such a diverse group of women. One might be surprised to find that included in this group of ten women were a pastor's wife, a doctor's wife, a country music star's wife, a single mom, a Hispanic girl from Brooklyn, a lady who had been raised in church, and a mother of a handicapped son.

When I look back on them, I have such gratitude and respect for the ten. They had the courage to come forward and deal with this painful part of their past when this class had not been tried and proven. Because of that courage they paved the way for others to come forward.

As of this writing, this study is still being taught at Cornerstone and has literally helped hundreds of women, and now men deal with past abortions.

I was so ecstatic with the group of women we had, I

hardly remember anything I said. I remember briefly telling my abortion story and allowing each woman in the circle to tell hers. Of course each story was different but yet so similar. Each tale included the same tragic circumstances that surround death. They told of the destructive lifestyle they all embraced after choosing abortion, and then the subsequent reasons for keeping this choice a secret. As the woman who had been raised in church was telling her story, she included the words, "If I could just save one unborn baby, I would tell my story." WOW! Those words again that I had heard in the studies taught in Chattanooga. I found it odd how they were spoken once again.

We made it almost all the way around the circle, but did not get to the woman I only recognized because I had noticed her pushing her son around the church campus in his wheelchair. She had started crying when she walked in the door and had not stopped the entire night. My heart broke for her remembering the anguish of facing this giant in my past. I was sure to get her number so I could contact her during the week. She needed to talk and I knew that. When I reached her she assured me she would return the next week and she would tell her story.

I spent that next week turning those familiar words over in my head, "If I could just save one, if I could just save one."

ALL 10 WOMEN

were present again the next week. Of course I had convinced myself that not one of them was coming back, but they did. I let the girl who didn't get to share the week before go first. She too told the tragic circumstances surrounding her abortion, and the subsequent reasons for keeping the secret. But one reason was different than any I had heard before. I will never forget what she said: "I told no one of my abortion because I didn't want them to look at my son in his wheelchair and think that was God's condemnation on my life." Just writing those words brings tears to my eyes. I felt like I had been punched in the stomach. I was so floored by them that I honestly don't remember much more of what she said. We dismissed on time and went to that evening's church service. All through church I kept hearing her say those words. I then realized why they upset me so badly.

If satan will use the most innocent of God's creation, a handicapped child, against his own mother, he will stop at nothing. That thought opened a new avenue of thinking about the lies satan told me, and was telling each of the ten women in the study, as well as the millions of men and women across our country. He has been allowed to roam freely among those who have made this choice and it was time to put a stop to it. I was fed up, heartbroken, enraged, and perplexed. What do I do about it? What can I, one woman, do about the most disastrous problem I believe we are facing in this country's history? The thought was overwhelming but yet I was plagued with the questions.

The following week we came together and had started getting in to the heart of the study. As one of the girls was talking she said, "I feel the same as 'Stacey', if it would just save one unborn baby, or save one woman from living in torment any longer, I would tell my story." Okay God, You have my attention. Someone then pointed out how it was funny that we kept hearing those words. I was thinking, yes funny, but no coincidence.

As you may have guessed by now I didn't get much rest during this twelve-week study. That week I again wrestled with the thoughts, the questions, my own conviction, and the dreams that brought me here in the first place. The bigger picture began to unfold over the coming weeks. If these women are willing to be vulnerable and tell their stories, then they need a platform to make that happen. I knew the world needed to hear what they had to say. The world needed to hear the truth.

THESE WOMEN'S LIVES

were changing. James tells us when we draw near to God, He will draw near to us. When God is near, change occurs. I wasn't doing anything magical to change their lives-God was. They had trusted me enough to share their most private secret and they were seeing changes in their lives because of their openness. They had become ten of my most intimate, dearest friends.

One particular Wednesday night I shared with the women all that God had been showing me over the weeks. I told them how those words that we kept hearing, I had already heard dozens of times in Chattanooga. I explained how the handicapped son story hit me hard. I expressed how I felt the world needed to hear their stories and the millions of other stories of people suffering after an abortion. I knew we needed to start a non-profit organization but I had no idea where to start.

That night the ten of us put our heads together and with God's help devised a plan. The country music star's wife, who had never experienced abortion but was there to support her girlfriend who had, already knew how to start a non-profit organization as she had not only started one, but was running it successfully. She was also the one to say the name of this organization had to be SaveOne. That was the perfect name. Everything was falling into place.

Throughout the duration of the twelve-week class and well into the next year, the ten of us downloaded documents, worded by-laws, submitted forms, and formed the first official board of directors. By early 2000 we had everything completed and got the approval that SaveOne was an official non-profit organization and we could start conducting business. We were so happy that our prayers and hard work had finally paid off.

It was during this time of formation I would occasionally drive across town to the local abortion mill and pray. I needed to be reminded why I was doing this and going there always prompted me and gave me such a sense of urgency. The day after I had been there praying I felt a nudging to return. I fought the urge, for I had much to do that day, but I finally succumbed and drove across town again to sit outside and pray. It was there God spoke to me as strongly as if He had been physically sitting in my car with me. He told me to open the Bible next to me and read Jeremiah 1:9-10. I opened the book and read these words: "For today I reached out my hand and touched your mouth and put my words in your mouth. For today I appoint you over nations and kingdoms, to uproot and tear down, to destroy and overthrow, to build and to plant."

Finally, the dreams made sense. I must speak boldly. I must tell others the truth. No one can argue with my personal experience. I began to see where God was leading us. Imagine if there were dozens, hundreds, thousands, and even tens of thousands of women and men healed and telling the truth about what this one choice did to change their lives forever. How many people would we save from its destruction and horrifying consequences? How many innocent children's lives would not be lost?

I COULD WRITE

another book about the ups and downs of running this organization. We have had our share of struggles, as well as our share of wonderful mountaintop experiences. We never tire of hearing the stories from men and women who come to us for help and certainly never tire of seeing that realization in their eyes that they too can be released from the prison abortion put them in. God is so good. I just can't say that enough.

Since the inception of SaveOne, I and different members of our staff have traveled to many states and countries sharing our stories in an effort to save one. We have been allowed to come into prisons, churches, pregnancy centers, and many other forums to start SaveOne chapters. By expanding this ministry and multiplying our knowledge, we become so much more effective. We're raising other men and women to tell their stories after God has performed a great healing in their lives.

Our staff has expanded to include regional and district chapter coordinators that cover every state in America. The first man who ever attended a SaveOne study has now, with the strong support and help of his wife, founded SaveOne Europe and is duplicating the philosophy of this ministry all across Europe.

When I think back to that broken girl who was intoxicated every weekend, I am in awe at how He has blessed my life. It is almost too much for me to comprehend. I am so thankful to God for taking the broken pieces of my life and turning it into a mosaic. Only God can do that. He can do it for you, too. A supernatural miracle is the only way to explain it.

I am thankful beyond words to the entire staff of SaveOne, the servants of the past, present, and future. Because of their willingness to be that "vessel of honor," God can flow through them to reach others and pull them out of the despair they're living in.

I know God is not finished with SaveOne. In fact, I

believe He has only just begun. He has called us to uproot, tear down, destroy, overthrow, build, and plant. We are doing just that in the lives of people everywhere. God is planting survivors of abortion as oaks of righteousness that He will build up to spread His truth.

HER NAME IS MEGHAN,

in case you're wondering. When I envision her today, I see a strong, vibrant young woman. I often wonder what she would be doing. As I go to weddings or attend funerals, I can't help but let my mind wonder how she would have impacted the scene: Would she be in this wedding as a bridesmaid? Was she supposed to be this bride's best friend? Has the bride missed out on someone who was supposed to affect her life because of my decision?

I watch my boys and can't keep from wondering how they would have grown up if they had an older sister as an example. Would they treat girls differently? What did they miss because of my choice more than two decades ago?

I look in to my husband's eyes and know he will never experience a daughter. How would being a dad of two boys and one girl have changed him? How would the dynamics of our family been different had we had a girl as a firstborn? These are all questions that will never be answered because of one choice I made over twenty years ago. They do not reflect my pain, but rather my regret that will plague me until the day I die.

I now picture the abortion wound as a scar that will forever be on my soul. Every wound leaves a scar so you always remember, but after it heals there's no longer pain from the wound. I will never forget what happened, and I will never stop regretting my choice, but I can now live my life without feeling the pain and shame abortion created.

That's what God did for me and it's what He can do for you.

YOU MAY BE ASKING

if I ever had the opportunity to talk to my old boyfriend "Brian" again. The answer is no. I have prayed on more than one occasion for God to cross our paths and allow me the privilege of asking for his forgiveness. I stole his fatherhood from him; a thought that haunts me to this day. If he had done the same to me he would have been ostracized, shunned, and called a deadbeat dad. I on the other hand am applauded for exercising my "right to choose". You can read between the lines of this paragraph and see the injustice to men in this situation.

We as a staff have dedicated ourselves to reaching out to men just as fervently as we do women. It's time they have a voice in this issue. It's a voice we're longing to hear.

One day I know I will come face to face with Meghan's father and it is my deep genuine and heartfelt prayer that I will find the words to express my sincere apology.

Until then we will continue to do everything in our power to make sure the man's voice is heard and they have a safe place to turn to and grieve.

I HOPE

as you have read my story of survival that you have developed a desire to take your own abortion story that satan meant for evil and allow God to turn it to good by helping others.

God's hand of favor and blessing is heavy upon the ministry of SaveOne. We would love for you to be a part of it.

If you are needing help recovering after abortion please go to www.saveone.org and click "Find a chapter near you". If one is not available in your area then please register for our online class. Regardless of the circumstances surrounding your experience, we want to help. We'll walk with you every step of the way.

Also, please contact us if you would like to start a chapter of SaveOne. A chapter allows you to teach the SaveOne study through your church, pregnancy center, or ministry. It's free, with no contracts to sign. We want to help you help others.

Chapter benefits include; monthly updates from our communications director; an easily accessible staff for answers to questions; a free web page on the SaveOne website; prayer support; access to chapter tools; and much more.

The SaveOne staff is also available for speaking engagements such as Pregnancy Resource Center banquets, church congregations, women's ministries, and pastor's functions.

We hope to hear from you soon!

SAVEONE
PO Box 291526
Nashville, TN 37229
www.saveone.org
www.saveoneeurope.org
866-329-3571

SaveOne: Our Mission

Our mission is to reach men and women suffering in silence after an abortion. Our passion is to help men and women reclaim and restore their peace of mind and self-worth.

Have you ever asked yourself any of these questions?
- Why am I an emotional wreck?
- Can I really overcome my guilt?
- Can I forgive her?
- Can I ever forgive myself?
- Will my depression ever end?
- What happened to my aborted child?
- Does God really care about me?

If you have . . . SaveOne offers help.

Together we can find the answers to these questions. We will help you *gain* control of your stray emotions, *free* yourself of guilt, *find* your source of courage, *renew* your mind, *experience* how far God's grace truly extends, and much more. *You can begin again!*

Hope for a new Beginning

"I felt I deserved death because I had more than one abortion. SaveOne cared and taught me that God loved me unconditionally in spite of my past." —Rachel

"I was my own prisoner." —Richard

"SaveOne told me I didn't have to deal with this memory alone anymore. The hardest thing I had to do was let the ladies of SaveOne love me. They showed me how to accept and give forgiveness. This, you may think is the end of the story; but I promise you it is really by the grace of God, only the beginning. With the help of SaveOne I now am one saved." —Angela

BE A PART OF CHANGING LIVES

Being on the front row as a witness of God's miracles is an amazing place to be. It's a better seat than front and center on Broadway, or the 50-yard line at the Super Bowl. Teaching the **SaveOne** curriculum gives you the best view of the miracles God is performing in men and women who are dealing with their abortion(s).

SaveOne works closely with ministries to establish chapters all around the world. A **SaveOne** chapter is simply a ministry (church, pregnancy center, etc.) that teaches the **SaveOne** curriculum. We have worked tirelessly to make becoming a chapter not only easy, but very beneficial to you and your ministry. As a chapter you have no membership fees to pay, no contracts to sign, plus you will receive a free web page within our website to direct people straight to you, a coordinator who is assigned to your state who will keep up with your needs, prayer requests, and be accessible to help you in whatever way we can. You will have access to "chapter tools" within our website which houses bulletin inserts, posters, links to available helps and more. We don't just leave you by yourself, but offer training and easy accessibility so you will know you are a part of a strong network of abortion recovery facilitators who are encouraging and praying for you on a regular basis.

SaveOne has been responsible for bringing dozens of families in to churches as well as clients and volunteers in to pregnancy centers. We have countless testimonies of lives changed from the inside out through the restoration of Jesus Christ. The people who come to you for help and find it are in turn so grateful and want to give back.

Come and sit on the front row with us and be a part of changing lives!

Men's curriculum   *Women's curriculum*

BOOKS ARE AVAILABLE FOR GROUP OR SELF-STUDY.

SaveOne Facilitator Training (DVD) is an easy to follow guide, teaching you how to conduct an abortion recovery class. The basic foundation for the class is restoration through Jesus Christ.

SaveOne's *May I Have This Dance?* will help you through your pregnancy. It is packed with insight and knowledge to help you make the journey an easier road to travel.

SaveOne's *The Survivor* is founder Sheila Harper's personal testimony.

CPSIA information can be obtained at www.ICGtesting.com
Printed in the USA
LVOW101947150313

324404LV00003B/7/P